D0996943

THE
SUN

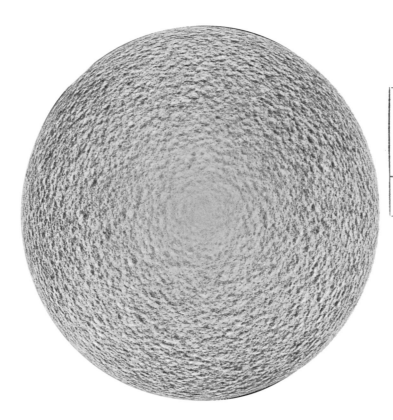

TIM FURNISS

WAYLAND

spinning through space

THE
SUN

Other titles in the series: The Earth ● The Moon ● The Solar System

Find Wayland on the Internet at http://www.wayland.co.uk

All Wayland books encourage children to read and help them improve their literacy.

✓ The contents page, page numbers, headings and index help locate specific pieces of information.

✓ The glossary reinforces alphabetic knowledge and extends vocabulary.

✓ The further information section suggests other books dealing with the same subject.

Cover photograph:
The spacecraft *Ulysses* travelled over the Sun's poles in 1994–5 [inset middle]; the spacecraft *SOHO* which stays in orbit around the Sun [inset left]; the aurora borealis [inset bottom]; the Sun's violent surface [main].

Title page: The Sun from *SOHO*, a spacecraft launched in 1996 to observe the Sun.

First published in 1999 by Wayland Publishers Limited,
61 Western Road, Hove, East Sussex, BN3 1JD, England

© Copyright 1999 Wayland Publishers Limited

Editor: Carron Brown
Designer: Tim Mayer
Production controller: Carol Titchener
Illustrator: Peter Bull

British Library in Cataloguing Publication Data
Furniss, Tim
   The Sun. – (Spinning through Space)
   1. Sun – Juvenile literature
   I. Title
   523.7

ISBN 0 7502 2407 X

Printed and bound in Italy by EuroGrafica, Vicenza.

CONTENTS

THE NEAREST STAR

The night sky twinkles with thousands of tiny lights; some are very faint and some are quite bright. On a clear night, when you look up into the sky, you are looking at about 2,500 stars.

During the day, the stars are still there but there is only one star that is bright enough to be seen during the day. This star is our Sun. It is about 150 million km away, which is just about the perfect distance. If the Sun was a bit closer, we would fry from the heat. If it was further away, we would freeze.

If the Sun was the size of a football, the Earth would be a pea 30 metres away.

The Sun shining bright in the Earth's sky. ▶

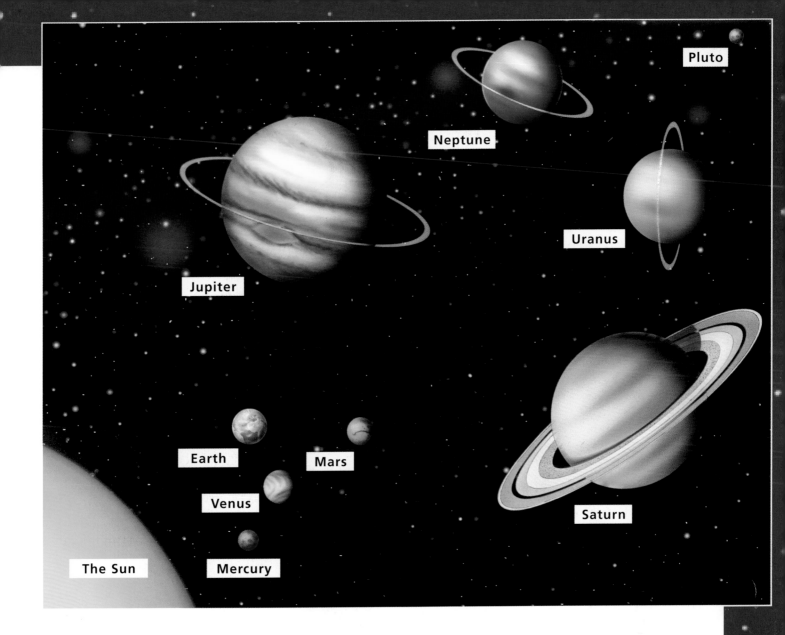

Pluto

Neptune

Uranus

Jupiter

Earth

Mars

Venus

Saturn

The Sun

Mercury

▲ The solar system. The nine planets orbit the Sun.

It takes light from the Sun 8 minutes and 17 seconds to reach the Earth.

Our planet, Earth, is one of nine planets that orbit the Sun. Mercury and Venus are the planets closest to the Sun. Then come Earth, Mars, Jupiter, Saturn, Uranus, Neptune and Pluto. Pluto, the smallest planet, is the furthest away from the Sun at a distance of 5,760 million km. From Pluto, the Sun would look like a small, bright star. Some planets have moons. The Earth has one moon. The Sun and its nine planets and their moons are called the solar system.

THE TINY SUN

The Sun and the stars that we can see are part of a galaxy. When you look into the night sky, you may be able to see part of our galaxy stretching above you like a long faint band of cloud, filled with the lights of over 100,000 million stars.

▼ The Milky Way, with the Sun's position arrowed.

We call this galaxy the Milky Way. The Milky Way is actually an inner arm of a spinning galaxy in space, called a spiral galaxy. From a distance, the Milky Way would look like the spiral made by a lit Catherine Wheel firework.

The Sun

The nearest star to the Sun is called Proxima Centauri. It takes light from this star 4.3 years to reach us. This is called 4.3 light years. The Sun is 270,000 times closer to us than Proxima Centauri.

The Sun is a very ordinary and small star compared with most of the stars in the Milky Way galaxy. The Milky Way is just one of millions of other galaxies in the vast universe. So, the Sun's place in the universe is very small and insignificant, but for us it is a vital life source. Without the Sun, our Earth would be a huge, dark, freezing lump of rock.

▼ The Sun compared with the surface of Betelgeuse, a red giant star in the Orion constellation. It is 300 times larger than the Sun. Its light takes 650 years to reach Earth.

SUN FACTS

The Sun is on an outer arm of the Milky Way, about 32,000 light years from the centre of the galaxy. Although the Sun is small compared with most of the stars in the universe, it looks big to us even though it is 150 million km away!

The Sun is so huge that 109 Earths would fit inside it. The diameter of the Sun around its equator is 1,392,000 km compared with the Earth's 12,800 km diameter, and it's 330,000 times heavier than Earth. The Sun contains 99.9% of the mass of the whole solar system.

The Sun takes 225 million years to orbit the Milky Way galaxy, travelling at a speed of 2,150 km per second.

▼ The burning Sun sets over the Pacific Ocean.

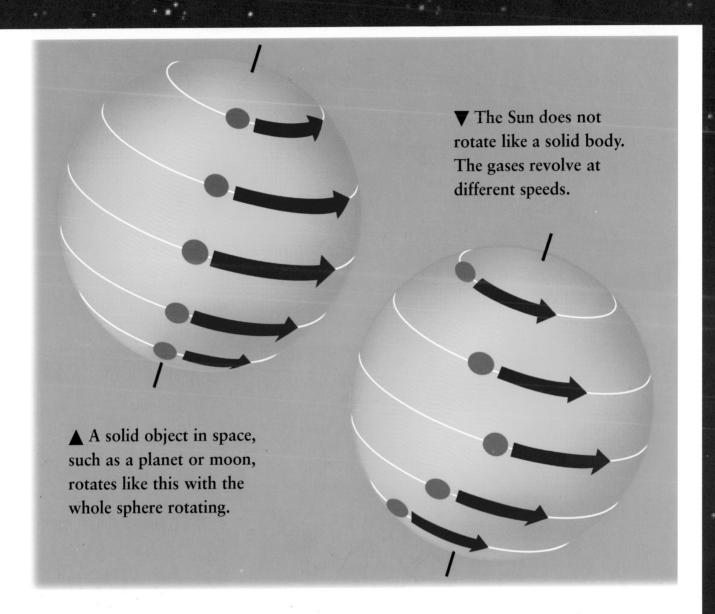

▼ The Sun does not rotate like a solid body. The gases revolve at different speeds.

▲ A solid object in space, such as a planet or moon, rotates like this with the whole sphere rotating.

The swirling sphere

Unlike Earth, which is a solid mass of rock, the Sun is a swirling, seething sphere of hot gases. Different areas of the Sun spin round at different speeds. The equatorial zones around the middle of the Sun make a full turn in 25 days. The polar regions at the top and bottom of the Sun spin around in 33 days.

The temperature at the centre of the Sun is 15 million°C but at the surface it is cooler, just 6,000°C.

The fiery heart of the solar system

The Sun produces most of the heat and energy in our solar system. The centre of the Sun is like a huge nuclear furnace. The temperature and pressure inside it are so high that they set off atomic reactions. Every second, 700 million tonnes of hydrogen fuse together to form helium. This process is called nuclear fusion. It releases enormous energy as heat and light.

The Sun's mass amounts to 4.5 million million million million tonnes.

▼ This is an X-ray photograph of the Sun showing its violent atmosphere at work.

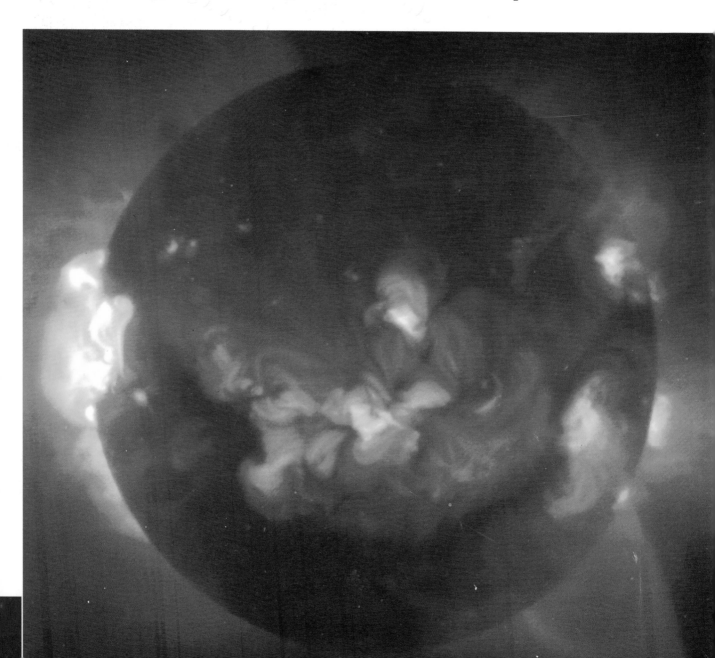

A star is formed out of a cloud of gas and dust. It begins to shine for millions of years before swelling up into a red giant and becoming a white dwarf star.

The dying Sun

The Sun's energy is slowly dying. It loses about 4 million tonnes of mass every second, which sounds a lot but it's really a very small amount compared to the Sun's total mass. Millions of years into the future, the Sun will run out of hydrogen. It will then expand and smother the whole solar system. Even then the Sun will not be totally destroyed; it will cool right down and become a tiny, weak star.

The Sun uses 22 million tonnes of hydrogen each year. Scientists have calculated that the Sun could go on shining for five billion years before it cools down.

THE SURFACE OF THE SUN

The Sun is a life-giving furnace. It is an ocean of fire and flame. Energy produced at the core of the Sun radiates out towards the surface.

Solar wind, the Sun's hot gas, can travel as far as Pluto, 5,900 million km away.

Layer upon layer of hot gas

The surface of the Sun is a seething mass of hydrogen gas, called the photosphere. The temperature ranges from 4,300°C to 9,000°C. The photosphere provides most of the light that comes from the Sun.

corona

energy radiating out

photosphere

core

chromosphere

◄ This cutaway diagram of the Sun shows the different layers of the star.

The upper level of the photosphere is called the chromosphere. This is a stormy region of very hot gases. Here, the temperatures rises to 1 million°C. The chromosphere is about 16,000 km thick.

Above the chromosphere, the Sun has a halo of even hotter gases called the corona. Some parts of the corona are 4 million°C. The outer layers of the corona are made up of hot gas blowing off from the Sun. This streams away from the Sun and is called the solar wind.

It is only possible to observe the chromosphere and corona from the Earth during a solar eclipse.

◀ Solar storms send atomic particles towards the Earth causing the aurora borealis.

◄ The Sun from *Skylab 4* space station showing some of the most spectacular prominences ever recorded.

Sunspots

Storms on the Sun can interfere with the Earth. Solar storms send out atomic particles that can destroy the Earth's upper atmosphere. These solar storms cause radio interference and aurorae, red and green glowing lights in the night sky.

The surface of the Sun can sometimes erupt with flame as energy escapes from its restless core to burst up through a sunspot. Sunspots are the dark patches that can be seen on the photosphere. They are the sites of violent storms caused by disturbances that dam up the flow of energy from inside the Sun. As a result, the bursts of hot energy can't reach the surface, which then becomes colder and therefore less bright. So they look almost black against the red-hot background of the Sun.

Sometimes, the sunspots release the energy, like a dam bursting. These sudden eruptions of gas cause flares to shoot out from the Sun's surface, like the fire from an angry dragon. These are called solar flares.

Prominences

Sometimes, huge, almost frightening, flames spurt from the Sun. These are called prominences. The prominences spurt out, like a huge fiery burp, without warning. There is a sudden uprush of energy from the Sun.

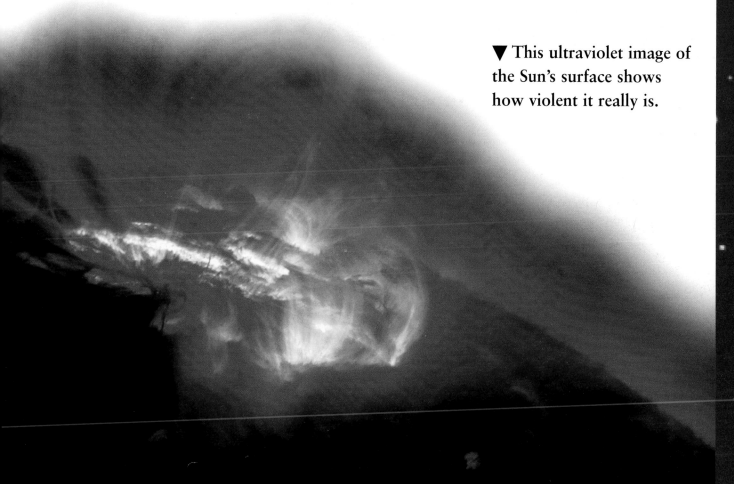

▼ This ultraviolet image of the Sun's surface shows how violent it really is.

THE SUN AND EARTH

The moving Sun?

The Sun appears to move across our sky: rising in the morning and setting at night. This is because the Earth is rotating or spinning around like a top as it orbits the Sun. This spinning means that the sky and everything we see in it appears to move. The Sun seems to rise in the east and set in the west. At about midday, the Sun is at its highest in the sky.

▼ The setting Sun photographed at 6-minute intervals at midsummer.

The Sun causes shadows. When the Sun is low in the sky, it casts long shadows. As it slowly climbs, the shadows get smaller because it is shining almost directly downwards. As the Sun moves, so do the shadows.

The Earth's axis is not perfectly upright as it orbits the Sun. It is inclined at an angle of 23.5 degrees. This tilt causes the seasons.

The seasons

Some parts of the Earth close to the North and South Poles do not experience sunlight during some weeks of the winter.

The tilting of the Earth causes the seasons. In the winter, the Sun seems to be lower in the sky and does not stay long. This is because your home is on the part of the Earth that is tilted away from the Sun. It is colder. During the summer, the Earth is tilted towards the Sun, so it is higher in the sky and stays for longer. Then it is hotter.

Not all parts of the Earth are at the same distance from the Sun at the same time. So when it's winter in the northern hemisphere, it's summer in the southern hemisphere, depending on which area is tilted towards the Sun.

▼ This artwork shows how the Earth's tilt causes the four seasons.

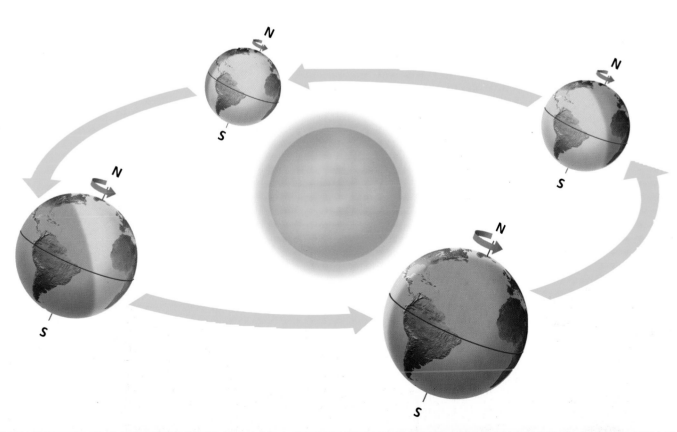

Radiation from the Sun

The Sun's energy is called radiation which travels in 'waves' of different lengths. Some of these waves form visible light that we can see. There are also shorter waves: gamma rays, ultraviolet light and X-rays. Infrared heat waves are longer and radio waves are longer still. Visible light comes almost in between. This radiation is called the electromagentic spectrum.

All radiation travels at 300,000 km per second. This is the same as the speed of light. Light is visible radiation.

▼ A rainbow is caused when the Sun's light is split into its different colours by the rain. These are called the colours of the spectrum.

The Earth's invisible shield

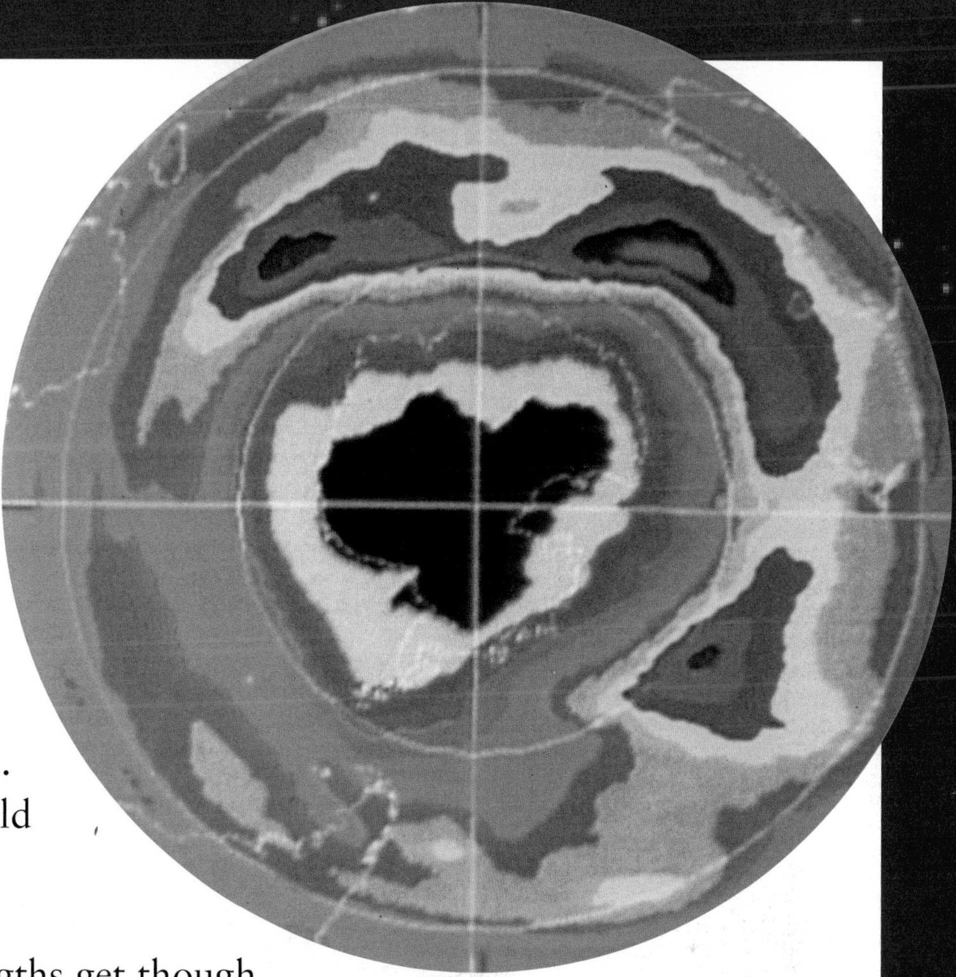

The amount of radiation reaching the Earth is only one two-thousandth-millionth of the Sun's output. The ozone layer in the atmosphere acts like an invisible shield stopping most of this radiation reaching the Earth's surface. Ultraviolet and X-rays would be very dangerous if they penetrated the atmosphere. Thankfully, visible wavelengths get though, bringing light to our unique planet.

Holes in the ozone layer!

The ozone layer is slowly being damaged by pollution. Scientists are worried that 'holes' in the ozone layer will let more damaging radiation in. The pollution is also causing carbon dioxide to increase the size of the atmosphere, creating the 'greenhouse effect' where heat from the Sun enters the atmosphere but cannot escape, causing our planet to warm up. Scientists are trying to work out how to help our planet cope.

▲ Satellites are able to keep watch on the development of holes in the ozone layer. One hole is shown here as the black patch in the centre.

Radiation does not come just from the Sun but from all over the universe.

Solar power

Radiation from the Sun provides us with light and warmth, making the Earth a world where life can exist. The Sun is free to us all. We don't have to pay for its light and heat. We can also use the Sun to provide us with power.

The Sun's energy can be converted into electricity using solar cells. Solar cells are used on satellites to provide electrical power. Thousands of small solar cells, looking like tiny mirrors, are assembled on panels attached to the satellite. These panels point at the Sun and

▲ Thousands of solar cells are assembled on panels attached to a satellite.

A typical communications satellite has two solar arrays which, like wings, span about 30 metres, generating 9 kW of electricity.

provide the power to make the spacecraft work. Solar cells have also used been used to power aircraft and cars.

Most solar cells use a reflective material called silicon, but new materials such as gallium arsenide are now being used because they can convert more of the Sun's energy to provide even more electrical power.

Another way of getting power from the Sun is called solar dynamics. Mirrors concentrate the Sun's light to boil water to steam, which drives turbines. These generate electricity.

▼ The solar cells on the roof of this house generate power to heat water.

Any way to generate power using the Sun's energy is good for the environment because it does not cause pollution in the atmosphere like power stations do.

SOLAR ECLIPSES

The Moon is much smaller than the Sun but it is a lot closer to the Earth so it seems big to us. The Moon sometimes passes in front of the Sun cutting out some or all of the Sun's light. This is called an eclipse.

▲ During an annular eclipse, the outer rim of the Sun can still be seen. 'Annular' means ring.

The longest solar eclipse seen was 7 minutes 8 seconds. Solar eclipses usually occur 2–3 times a year. Visit the websites on page 31 to look out for future eclipses.

A total eclipse occurs when the Moon passes across and covers the Sun completely. This produces a deep shadow that reaches a small part of the Earth. Inside this shadow, an observer experiences one of the most dramatic sights anybody can see – the total eclipse. Outside this shadow, the Moon cuts out only part of the Sun and, as some of the Sun can be seen, it does not get so dark. The observer sees a partial eclipse.

By flying an aircraft to keep up with the movement of the Moon that creates the eclipse, some astronomers managed to experience a total eclipse lasting 72 minutes.

Another eclipse is called an annular eclipse. This is when the Moon looks slightly smaller at its furthest point from the Earth and passes in front of the Sun. The outer rim of the Sun can still be seen during this eclipse.

◄ A photograph of a total eclipse taken on 11 July 1991, Mexico.

SPACECRAFT EXPLORERS

If we flew too close to the Sun, we would fry. No spacecraft has been able to get very close. Some unmanned spacecraft have been launched to observe the Sun from a safe distance in orbit around it. Two *Helios* spacecraft were launched into solar orbit in 1975. They came to within 48 million km of the Sun. The *Helios* twins survived temperatures hot enough to melt lead.

▼ SOHO took this image of the Sun's surface showing that it is constantly changing.

The *Helios* probes reached a record speed of 254,000 km per hour.

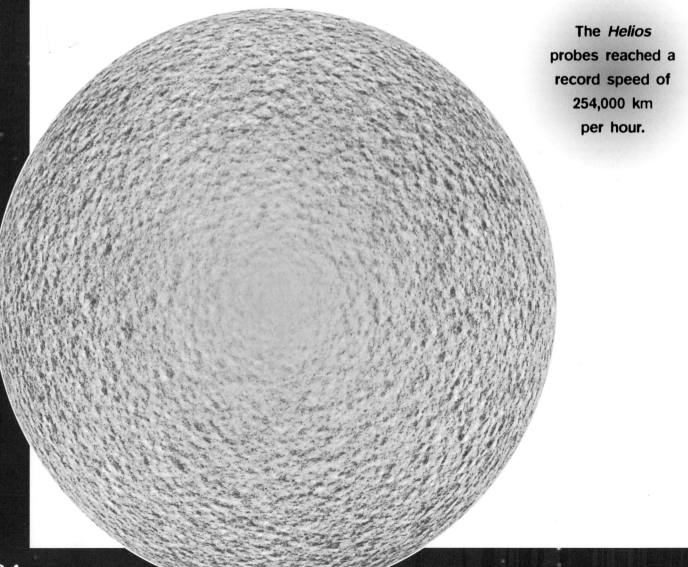

◀ The European *SOHO* keeps a constant eye on the Sun.

Many satellites in orbit around the Earth keep watch on the radiation coming from the Sun. Some satellites are used to warn the Earth about a strong burst of radiation coming from the Sun. This can cause interference in the atmosphere and to radio transmissions.

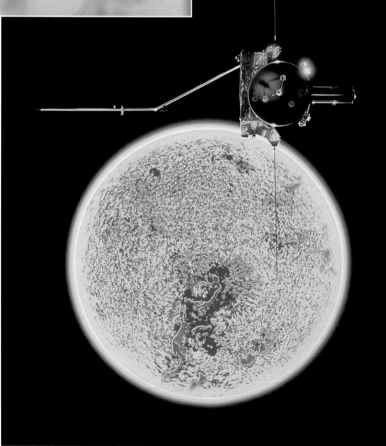

A European spacecraft called the *Solar and Heliospheric Observatory* or *SOHO* was launched to study the Sun in 1996. It was placed into a special orbit between the Earth and the Sun. *SOHO* points at the Sun all the time. It has sent back amazing images of the surface of the Sun. Other pictures show solar flares and prominences. One spacecraft flew over the Sun's poles in 1994–5. It was named *Ulysses*.

▲ *Ulysses* travelled at a speed of 51,682 km per hour to break free from Earth's gravity.

OBSERVING THE SUN

It is very dangerous to look at the Sun! Never look at the Sun through binoculars or a telescope. You will be immediately blinded by its heat and light!

The Sun can only be observed safely by using a piece of white card at the end of the telescope. The telescope then projects an image of the Sun on to the card. This must only be done under supervision. Point the telescope towards the area of the sky where the Sun is. A cap must be placed over the eye lens. Hold a card about 50 cm away from the end of the telescope. Take the cap off the lens. Move the telescope to and fro and you will soon find that the Sun's image is on the card. Using this method, it may be possible to see sunspots.

The first observation of a sunspot was made in China, in 28 BC!

Most of the Kitt Peak telescope is underground. A cool, constant temperature makes sure that the delicate scientific instruments can work perfectly. ▶

Special telescopes and observatories have been built on the Earth to observe the Sun. One of the most famous is at Kitt Peak, Arizona, in the USA. This observes the Sun in the same way that we can using an ordinary telescope. The image of the Sun that the Kitt Peak observatory can project is much bigger. It allows astronomers to see the actual surface of the Sun.

▲ Keep away from the lens at the end of the telescope and observe the Sun safely with card, like this.

TOPIC WEB

MATHS
- Measurement: e.g., diameter, distance from the planets.
- Compare the sizes of the Sun to the Moon and the nine planets in the solar system.

ART AND CRAFT
- History of art: look at how the Sun has been drawn and painted through history in different parts of the world.
- Draw or paint a picture of the Sun, drawing in sunspots, flares and restless gaseous surface.

DESIGN AND TECHNOLOGY
- Make a sundial using a round base with a pencil in the middle. Record the different times using the Earth's shadow.
- Look at how solar panels are designed for use on buildings and satellite and how they generate power.

MUSIC
- Compose a piece of music that describes the restless, exploding surface of the Sun.

THE SUN

HISTORY
- Find out about what people thought about the Sun in the past: e.g., through myths and legends.

ENGLISH
- Write a poem that will help you remember the colours of a rainbow.
- Imagine that you are the first person to come close to the Sun in a spacecraft. Write a newspaper report that describes what you felt.

SCIENCE
- Record the length of shadows at different times of the day to show the Earth's movement around the Sun.
- Investigate day and night at different times of the year.
- Think about the different sources of light we have. Which ones are natural and what do the others use in order to work?

GEOGRAPHY
- Look at the world on a globe. Figure out what times and seasons different countries have.
- Environmental change: Sun's radiation, the ozone layer and the greenhouse effect; solar power and its advantages and disadvantages.
- How solar storms effect the Earth. Where are the aurora borealis seen and at what time of year?

NOTES FOR TEACHERS

Chapter 1 – The nearest star

Recreate a solar system in the classroom and imagine the outer limits outside. The Sun is a football. The Earth is 30 m away but Pluto is the pip of an apple 1.6 km away! Think of a landmark that is about that distance from the school.

Chapter 2 – The tiny Sun

Refer to a simple star map and, if possible, arrange for the pupils to spot some of the most famous and brightest stars, to create the understanding of the vastness of the universe.

Chapter 3 – Sun facts

Create a simple but very high bar chart showing dramatically, the highest temperature on the Earth (58°C) and the hottest part of the Sun (6,000°C).

Chapter 4 – The surface of the Sun

The storms on the Sun's surface can cause aurora borealis. Investigate further into this phenomenon finding out where and when it occurs and look at the patterns they create.

Chapter 5 – The Sun and Earth

• Ask the pupils to look up at an object on the ceiling in front of them and walk forwards, to see the object 'move' across the ceiling.

• Like a prism, a rainbow is a perfect demonstration of the visible light spectrum, showing its different colours. Ask the children to make up a rhyme to remember the different colours.

• Make a sundial. Start with a round base and place a pencil or stick vertically in the middle. At each hour of the day mark where the shadow lies on the base.

• Investigate buildings that have solar electricity generators or solar panels. There might be one near the school. Look at the different designs that are used and their advantages and disadvantages.

Chapter 6 – Solar eclipses

Demonstrate a solar eclipse using a lamp and a ball of the same size of the inside of the lampshade. The lampshade and bulb can be shone at the pupils and the ball can be moved across its front.

Chapter 7 – Observing the Sun

• Ask a local astronomical society to arrange to demonstrate the safe way of observing the Sun.

• Look on the Internet using the websites on page 31. There are regular updates on the Sun's surface and a visual tour of the Sun. Altogether a very safe way of observing our nearest star.

GLOSSARY

Astronomers People who study space.

Atoms The smallest possible part of something, such as a gas.

Constellation A group of stars that we can see in the same area in the night sky. They may not be in the same galaxy.

Core The central part of something.

Equator The imaginary line around the middle of a planet or star, halfway between the polar regions.

Flares Sudden bursts of flame.

Galaxy A group of millions or billions of stars in the sky.

Gravity A force that brings smaller objcts closer to larger objects.

Hemisphere Half of a sphere. The Earth is split up into two spheres, called the northern and the southern hemispheres.

Hydrogen An invisible gas with no colour or smell.

Nuclear Energy that is emitted from reactions involving atoms.

Observatory A place from which astronomers study space, usually with powerful telescopes.

Orbit To go round.

Ozone layer A protective layer of gas in the Earth's atmosphere that absorbs harmful radiation from the Sun.

Planet A solid, spherical mass in space that orbits a star.

Polar regions The very north and south of a planet or star, more commonly known as the North Pole and the South Pole.

Probes Unmanned spacecraft that are equipped to find out information about space and transmit it back to Earth.

Prominences Eruptions of energy and flame from the Sun that fall back down to the surface.

Radiation Energy transmitted invisibly as electromagnetic waves. There are many different types of radiation.

Stars Large, luminous points in space that are spherical and made up of many different gases.

Turbines Types of wheel powered by water or steam that drive engines and create power.

Universe Everything that is in space.

FURTHER INFORMATION

Web sites:

www.astro.uva.nl~michielb/od95/
You can explore the Sun on this virtual tour.

sohowww.nascom.nasa.gov/ This site has the latest news on the Sun direct from SOHO.

starchild.gsfc.nasa.gov/ This site is geared towards young people with an interest in astronomy. You can find out Sun facts as well as looking deeper into space.

Books:

A Closer Look at The Ozone Hole by Alex Edmonds (Watts, 1996)

I didn't know that the Sun is a Star by Kate Petty (Watts, 1997)

The Gobsmacking Galaxy by Kjartan Poskitt (Scholastic, 1997)

The Kingfisher Book of Space by Martin Redfern (Kingfisher, 1998)

Sun and Moon by Patrick Moore (Riverswift, 1996)

Why do we have different seasons? and *What is an eclipse?(Ask Isaac Asimov* series) (Heinemann, 1994)

Places to visit:

The Science Museum, Exhibition Road, South Kensington, London (Tel: 0171 938 8000) has many exhibits about rockets, satellites and other spacecraft.

The Planetarium, Euston Road, London (Tel: 0171 935 6861) has programmes about planets, space and the stars, and how they are explored by spacecraft and satellites.

Picture acknowledgements:

The publishers would like to thank the following for allowing us to reproduce their pictures in this book: Bruce Coleman Ltd 2, 14, /Johnny Johnson *cover* [bottom], 13, /S. Nielsen 4, /Kim Taylor 16; Eye Ubiquitous /John Hulme 21; Genesis Photo Library *cover* [middle], *title page*, 19, 25 (bottom), /ESM 25, /NASDA, Japan 10; Popperfoto 18; Science Photo Library/J. Baum & N. Henbest 6, /Dr Fred Espenale 23, /David Hardy 12, /Ton Kinsberen *cover* [top], 25 (top), /NASA *contents page*, *cover* [main], 15, /David Parker 26, /Pekka Parviainen 8; Topham/Jerry Saxon 22; Wayland Picture Library/Telefocus 20.

The illustrations on pages 5, 7, 9, 11, 17 and 27 are by Peter Bull.

INDEX

All numbers in **bold** refer to pictures as well as text.